STRONG SISTERS OF STRENGTH™

PRESENTS:

Intentional Prayer

STRONG SISTERS OF STRENGTH™

PRESENTS:

Intentional Prayer

28 Day Devotional

Dr. Cecilia Denise Wilson Smith

XULON PRESS

Xulon Press
2301 Lucien Way #415
Maitland, FL 32751
407.339.4217
www.xulonpress.com

ISBN-13: 978-1-6628-6991-4

Dedication

This book is dedicated to my Husband, my Strong Sisters of Strength™, and every person that will use this Prayer Devotional to intentionally include prayer in their daily ritual. A special Thank you to Rev. Monica, Elder Angela, and Felita for accompanying me on this book journey.

Table of Contents

Introduction

If we intercede like never before, God will intervene like never before. I cannot imagine my life in this season without prayer and devotion in it. I purposely start each day praying and end every day praying. I stand on the scripture that states "men ought to always pray and not faint". I can't even begin to tell you the countless blessings that have been bestowed upon me simply by praying, asking, seeking, and knocking. My sincere prayer for you, is that you as the reader, find it important to include prayer at the beginning, throughout and at the end of your day. Prayer does not just happen. I have learned to intentionally pray about everything.

CHAPTER 1

Trust

Scripture:

"Trust in the LORD with all thine heart; And lean not unto thine own understanding. In all thy ways acknowledge him, and he shall direct thy paths." Proverbs 3:5-6 KJV

Reflections:

To trust God is to demonstrate a firm belief in his reliability, truth, and strength. Even when I am unreliable, he is reliable. God has an impeccable track record. My understanding is not as concise as God's understanding. I intend to keep trusting him as he leads me on this journey called life.

Question:

Who or What is it that you need to trust God with today?

_____

_____

_____

_____

My prayer:

Dear God,
I Trust in you with all my heart; And I choose to lean not on My own understanding. Lord In all my ways, I acknowledge you. Why, because you will direct my paths. In a world filled with people I cannot trust; I am grateful I can trust you. I am grateful I can trust you with all my heart with no regrets. I am grateful I can still acknowledge you and I can still do what you ask of me. Lord, I know you will never leave me or abandon me. Not because of who I am, but because of who you are. Thank you, Lord. I ask this prayer in Jesus' name, Amen.

Write Your thoughts:

_____

_____

_____

_____

Affirmation: I will trust in the Lord with all my heart.

CHAPTER 2

Need

Scripture:

"The LORD is my shepherd; I shall not want." Psalm 23:1 KJV

Reflections:

The Lord is everything I need in this life. He is still the answer to every one of my questions I am seeking clarity on. The Lord is my beginning and my end. He's everything to me. I want for nothing.

Question:

What is it that you need God to do for you?

_____

_____

_____

_____

My Prayer:

Dear God,
I'm grateful you are my Lord. I'm grateful for your grace and mercy you show me. I've learned to never forget who you have called me to be. I ask this prayer in Jesus' name, amen.

Write your thoughts:

_____

_____

_____

Affirmation: I want for nothing.

CHAPTER 3

Scripture:

> "Also, I heard the voice of the Lord, saying, whom shall I send, and who will go for us? Then said I, here am I; send me." Isaiah 6:8 KJV

Reflections:

> "Jesus said to his disciples, 'The harvest is great, but the workers are few.'" Matthew 9:37 NLT

I'm willing and able to be the hands and feet of Jesus. I can and I will go wherever I'm sent to help the people of God. In this season, there are so many needs. And so few people willing to help others.

Question:

Will you go where he is sending you today? Why or why not?

_____

_____

_____

My Prayer:

Dear God, I hear your voice saying, whom shall I send, and who will go for us? Lord, I say, "Here am I; send me". Lord, I have no hesitation. I am ready to go for you. I know you've equipped me to go. Strengthen me for my journey. Protect me in this season. I ask this prayer in Jesus' name. Amen.

Write your thoughts:

_____

_____

_____

_____

_____

_____

_____

Affirmation: I can and will GO wherever he sends me.

CHAPTER 4

I Know

Scripture:

"And we are confident that he hears us whenever we ask for anything that pleases him. And since we know he hears us when we make our requests, we also know that he will give us what we ask for." 1 John 5:14-15 NLT

Reflections:

Some things in this life I just know. As uncertain as life can be, I'm certain God hears my prayers. My challenge is to not grow weary while doing good, for in due season we shall reap if we do not lose heart. (Galatians 6:9 NKJV)

Question:

What things are you certain of in this life:

_____

_____

_____

_____

_____

_____

My Prayer:

Dear God,

I'm confident that you hear us whenever we ask for anything that pleases you. And since we know you hear us when we make our requests, we also know that you will give us what we ask for. My challenge God is to pray and stay connected to you. Then I will know what to ask that pleases you. I ask this prayer in Jesus' name. Amen.

Write your thoughts:

_____

_____

_____

_____

_____

_____

Affirmation: I am confident that God hears me.

CHAPTER 5

It's Possible

Scripture:

"He replied, "What is impossible for people is possible with God." Luke 18:27 NLT

Reflections:

So many times, in my life I felt helpless to address my current situation. As much as I had done everything I knew to do, I still came up short. At that point, is when I realize, it is not in me to solve my issue. However, God the Father specialize in hopeless and helpless situations. Anything is possible with God. I am challenged to surrender and remember who God is, no matter how many times I fall short and miss the mark.

Question:

What is that you need to turn over to God knowing all things are possible with Him?

_____

_____

_____

_____

My Prayer:

Dear God,
Thank you for teaching me "What is impossible for me is
extremely possible with you." Thank you for allowing me to
live long enough to learn my limitations and realize you have
no limitations. I ask this prayer in Jesus' name, Amen.

Write Your thoughts:

_____

_____

_____

_____

_____

_____

Affirmation: What is impossible for me, is possible with God.

CHAPTER 6

Walk

Scripture:

"For we walk by faith, not by sight." II Corinthians 5:7
NKJV

Reflections:

In this life, I have walked many paths simply paying attention to what was directly in front of me. Sometimes what was in front of me distracted me from my destination. It wasn't until I learned to walk by faith, that I realized, it didn't matter what was in front of me. My faith allows me to see past my obstacles on my way to my destiny. Obstacles will always be around. My faith will always keep me focused on what is most important. My faith will remind me to prepare to move past anything blocking my way. I intentionally look past roadblocks to see what is next.

Questions:

How is your walk? What do you see? Are you still moving?

_____

_____

My Prayer:

Dear God,
I am so grateful to have opportunity to walk by faith and not by sight. When I walk by faith, I see you all along my way. That truly helps me keep moving. Thank you, God, for focus and strength. I ask this prayer in Jesus' name, amen.

Write your thoughts:

_____

_____

_____

_____

Affirmation: I walk by faith and not by sight.

CHAPTER 7

Instructions

Scripture:

""At that time, I instructed the judges, 'You must hear the
cases of your fellow Israelites and the foreigners living
among you. Be perfectly fair in your decisions and impar-
tial in your judgments. Hear the cases of those who are
poor as well as those who are rich. Don't be afraid of anyone's anger, for the decision you make is God's decision.
Bring me any cases that are too difficult for you, and I will
handle them.'"At that time, I gave you instructions about
everything you were to do." Deuteronomy 1:16-18 NLT

Reflections:

The Bible is full of instructions even for judges. God leaves
no gray area. Every instruction he provides is specific and
intentional yielding the results needed.

Question:

What instructions do you need to seek God for?

_____

_____

My Prayer:

Dear God,
Thank you for consistently providing the instructions we need to live according to your plan for our lives. Lord, remind me on days when I do not stop to ask you as I should always do. God I am grateful I still have opportunity to come to you for instructions. I ask this prayer in your son Jesus name, amen.

Write your thoughts:

_____

_____

_____

Affirmation: I follow God's instructions.

CHAPTER 8

Praying for Others

Scripture:

"Ever since I first heard of your strong faith in the Lord
Jesus and your love for God's people everywhere, I have not
stopped thanking God for you. I pray for you constantly,
asking God, the glorious Father of our Lord Jesus Christ,
to give you spiritual wisdom and insight so that you might
grow in your knowledge of God. I pray that your hearts
will be flooded with light so that you can understand the
confident hope he has given to those he called—his holy
people who are his rich and glorious inheritance. I also
pray that you will understand the incredible greatness of
God's power for us who believe him. This is the same
mighty power that raised Christ from the dead and seated
him in the place of honor at God's right hand in the heav-
enly realms." Ephesians 1:15-20 NLT

Reflections:

As I have matured in Christ, I have learned to pray
past my own needs. I am honored to intercede for so
many believing God for so much. I pray first for their spiritual wisdom and insight so they may grow in the knowledge of who God is. So many people have no idea who God

has called them to be in this life. I am convinced if more Christians knew of their rich and glorious inheritance, they would easily understand the incredible greatness of God's power for all believers.

Question:

How often do you pray for other believers?

_____

_____

_____

_____

_____

_____

_____

_____

My Prayer:

Dear God,

Today I pray that each believer possesses strong faith and love for all Christians in this world. We shall never know the extent to which our prayers are spread for so many believers. I will continue to pray constantly for spiritual wisdom and continued growth in each believer. I ask this prayer in Jesus' name, amen.

Write your thoughts:

_____

_____

_____

_____

_____

_____

Affirmation: I consistently pray for the needs of others.

CHAPTER 9

The Search

Scripture:

"Search me, God, and know my heart; test me and know my anxious thoughts. See if there is any offensive way in me and lead me in the way everlasting." Psalm 139:23-24

Reflections:

My sincere desire is to be in the right position with God. I want to be available for God to use me. I want my heart to be available to be used by God. As I consistently study God's word, my desire is to align my life according to his word.

My Prayer:

Dear God,
My sincere desire is for you to search me and know my heart. Lord, I want to be able to be used by you for your glory. Please allow my life to be a testimony worth sharing with others. I ask this prayer in Jesus' name, amen.

Write your Thoughts:

_____

_____

_____

_____

_____

_____

Affirmation: I am available to be used by God.

CHAPTER 10

Gifts

Scripture:

> "Each of you should use whatever gift you have received
> to serve others, as faithful stewards of God's grace in its
> various forms." 1 Peter 4:10 NIV

Reflections:

The moment I realized my gifts were not so much for
me as they were to be used to benefit others, my whole
life shifted.

My Prayer:

Dear God, I am so grateful I have learned to use my gifts to
serve others. I am learning to be a faithful steward of my gifts
and your grace. It's so humbling to be used by you. I ask this
prayer in Jesus' name, amen.

Write your thoughts:

_____

_____

_____

_____

_____

_____

Affirmation: I use my gifts to serve others.

CHAPTER 11

Thank You

Scripture:

"Give thanks to the Lord, for He is good! His faithful love
endures forever. Who can list the glorious miracles of the
Lord? Who can ever praise Him enough?" Psalm 106:1–2

Reflections:

Before I complain at all, I've learned to give thanks. I have
many disappointments and setbacks. However, I have
just as many praise reports. No matter what I face, I am consistently reminded of how good God is to me.

Question:

How else can you thank God?

_____

_____

_____

_____

_____

_____

My prayer:

Dear God, I've learned to stop daily to give you thanks because you are so good! I know your faithful love endures even when I've sometimes given up. Today I'm thankful for your grace and mercy towards me. I ask this prayer in Jesus' name, amen.

Write your thoughts:

_____

_____

_____

_____

_____

_____

Affirmation: I give thanks to the Lord because he is good.

CHAPTER 12

Devote

Scripture:

"Devote yourselves to prayer, being watchful and thankful."
Colossians 4:2 NIV

Reflections:

Once I learned prayer is mandatory instead of optional, my perspective changed. Rather than remembering to pray in crisis, I learned to pray continually about everything and everybody. I have become loyal and committed to praying by searching for all opportunities to pray.

Question:

What are you devoted to?

_____

_____

_____

_____

My prayer:

Dear God, I'm grateful that I've learned to be Devoted to prayer, by being watchful and thankful for all you do for me. It's not an automatic action. I am intentionally focused on constant communication with you. I ask this prayer in Jesus' name amen.

Write your thoughts:

_____

_____

_____

_____

_____

_____

Affirmation: I am devoted to prayer.

CHAPTER 13

Say It

Scripture:

> "So, Jesus said to them, "Because of your unbelief; for
> assuredly, I say to you, if you have faith as a mustard seed,
> you will say to this mountain, move from here to there,
> and it will move; and nothing will be impossible for you."
> Matthew 17:20

Reflections:

I do not remember a time when I did not know how important my voice was. I have learned each of us have a unique voice that expresses who we are. There is so much power in our voice and the words that come from our mouth. I could not be me without my voice. My voice allows me to share my thoughts. My voice allows me to be heard. Each of us have a voice to help ourselves and others. Even if we don't have the right words, God always empower us with what we need to say. All we need do is seek his wisdom to use our voice.

Question:

What do you need to say?

_____

_____

_____

My Prayer:

Dear God, please help my unbelief. Help me stay focused enough to build my faith through every one of my trials you have continued to sustain me through. Remind me to use my voice to speak to every one of my mountains to remind me that you said **nothing** will be impossible to me. I ask this prayer in Jesus' name, amen.

Write your thoughts:

_____

_____

_____

Affirmation: I have the faith to speak to my mountains and I believe they will move.

CHAPTER 14

Stand Firm

Scripture:

> "A final word: Be strong in the Lord and in his mighty power. Put on all of God's armor so that you will be able to stand firm against all strategies of the devil." Ephesians 6:10-11 NLT

Reflections:

I've had some weary days that have left me drained of my strength. At that point is when I rely on my strength in the Lord. This life has taught me to put on all of God's armor so that I'm not so apt to collapse under the pressure of the many strategies and distractions of the devil. The devil is disguised in so many ways. My prayer life has strengthened my discernment to ensure I see Satan coming.

Reminder:

Put on the whole armor of God when you rise each day.

My Prayer:

Dear God, help me to Become strong in the Lord and in your mighty power. Keep reminding me to wear your armor, so that I will stand firm against all strategies of the devil. I ask this prayer in your son's name. Amen.

Write your thoughts:

_____

_____

_____

_____

_____

_____

Affirmation: Each day, I Put on all of God's armor so that I will be able to stand firm against all the tricks of the devil.

CHAPTER 15

Scripture:

> "People may be pure in their own eyes, but the Lord examines their motives. Commit your actions to the Lord, and your plans will succeed." Proverbs 16:2-3 NLT

Reflections:

Most times, I simply see what I see. I see what is right in front of me. However, God examines me, and my motives and He sees past me. He sees my heart and my motives. His examination of me shows me myself. That's the me I must work on daily. That's the me that I desire to show and do what he has called me to do in this season.

Question:

What does the Lord see when he examines you?

_____

_____

_____

My Prayer:

Dear God,
While I may see me one way, I know you examine me and my motives. Lord, please help me continue to desire to be everything you have called me to be in this life. Lord, please help me commit all my actions to you so that all my plans will succeed. I ask this prayer in Jesus' name. Amen.

Write your thoughts:

_____

_____

_____

Affirmation: I will Commit all my actions to the Lord, so all my plans will succeed.

CHAPTER 16

Keep Asking

Scripture:

> "So, I say to you, ask, and it will be given to you; seek, and you will find; knock, and it will be opened to you. For everyone who asks receives, and he who seek finds, and to him who knocks it will be opened." Luke 11:9-10

Reflections:

I have learned just because I do not get what I prayed for immediately, does not mean my prayer is not answered. Normally the delay is for my good and for his glory. My timetable may not match my destiny. However, my faith has grown enough to know I can keep praying knowing what his will is will be revealed in his timing.

Question:

What are you still praying about?

_____

_____

_____

My Prayer:

Dear God,
I am grateful I know I can keep asking, keep seeking, and keep knocking as I petition your throne for my desires. I know, if I keep praying, you will reveal to me your will and your way for me. I ask this prayer in your son Jesus name, amen.

Write your thoughts:

_____

_____

_____

_____

_____

Affirmation: I will keep asking, seeking, and knocking.

CHAPTER 17

What do You Want?

Scripture:

> "Now a certain man was there who had an infirmity thirty-eight years. When Jesus saw him lying there, and knew that he already had been in that condition a long time, He said to him, "Do you want to be made well?"" John 5:5-6 NKJV

Reflections:

M any times, we do not get what we want because we do not know what we want. I encourage you to take some time and really search your heart to determine what do you want God to do for you. What do you want? Do you know? Is where you are now, where you want to be? Try not to become so caught up in your current circumstances that you forget what your heart's desire is. Be prepared to share your desires with God in prayer.

Question:

Do you want to be made well?

_____

_____

_____

My Prayer:

Dear God,
Help me self-assess my current situation, so I can easily determine what I want and need for you to do for me. Lord my
sincere desire is to be made whole and well. Help me see what
you see in me Lord. I ask this prayer in Jesus' name, amen.

Write your thoughts:

_____

_____

_____

Affirmation: I want to be whole and well.

He Sees You

Scripture:

"And behold, there was a woman who had a spirit of infirmity eighteen years and was bent over and could in no way raise herself up. But when Jesus saw her, He called her to Him and said to her, "Woman, you are loosed from your infirmity." And He laid His hands on her, and immediately she was made straight, and glorified God." Luke 13:11-13 NKJV

Reflections:

Many times, in this life, you may feel unseen by people. Today just know God sees you. No matter where you are and where you have been, God sees you. It does not matter how many people are around you, he sees you.

Question:

God sees you. Do you see Him in your life?

_____

_____

My Prayer:

Dear God,
Thank you for seeing me. Thank you for calling me to you.
Thank you for healing and delivering me from me. I ask this
prayer in your son Jesus name, amen.

Write your thoughts:

_____

_____

_____

_____

_____

_____

Affirmation: God sees me.

CHAPTER 19

Who?

Scripture:

> "What then shall we say to these things? If God is for us,
> who can be against us?" Romans 8:31 NKJV

Reflections:

I have spent a part of my life trying to figure out who is for me and who is not. Imagine my surprise to realize it really does not matter. It is good to know who Jesus is. It is good to know HE is for me. Thus, whomever else is against me is against me.

Just a Thought:

You have everything you need in the word of God.

My Prayer:

Dear Lord, thank you for allowing me to regain the time I have lost being concerned about who is for me. Today I know because you are for me, it does not matter who is not for me. Thank you. I ask this prayer in Jesus' name, Amen.

Write your thoughts

_____

_____

_____

_____

_____

_____

Affirmation: God is for me. It does not matter who is against me.

CHAPTER 20

Confidence

Scripture:

"Being confident of this very thing, that He who has begun
a good work in you will complete it until the day of Jesus
Christ;" Philippians 1:6 NKJV

Reflections:

Confidence is defined as the feeling or belief that one
can rely on someone or something (Firm trust). I have
complete confidence that the Lord is not done with me just
yet. Knowing that fact helps me give myself grace for all my
mistakes and mishaps. I believe he created me for purpose.
My purpose is still being confirmed and evolved because I
am still here.

My Prayer:

Dear God,
I am confident that you are still allowing me to become who
you have called me to be. I am confident that you believe I am
a good work in progress. I ask this prayer in Jesus' name, amen.

Write your Prayer:

_____

_____

_____

_____

_____

_____

Affirmations: He that has begun a good work in me, will complete it. He is still using me for his glory.

Scripture:

"Rejoice in the Lord always. Again, I will say, rejoice!"
Philippians 4:4 NKJV

Reflections:

Rejoice: To feel or show great joy or delight. I have learned to rejoice in the goodness of who God is. He is good and he is God. In the good and bad, he is still good.

My Prayer:

Dear God, I will rejoice in you always. In the midst of it all, I choose to rejoice. I ask this prayer in Jesus' name, amen.

Write your thoughts:

_____

_____

_____

_____

_____

_____

Affirmation: I will always rejoice in the Lord.

CHAPTER 22

Fix My Mind

Scripture:

> "And now, dear brothers and sisters, one final thing. Fix your
> thoughts on what is true, and honorable, and right, and
> pure, and lovely, and admirable. Think about things that
> are excellent and worthy of praise." Philippians 4:8 NLT

Reflections:

To focus is to fix my mind on what matters and what is
most important. Fix my mind on what will matter in this
life and not the temporary distractions.

My Prayer:

Dear God, please help me focus on what matters to you. Help
me fix my thoughts on what is true, honorable, right, pure,
lovely, and admirable. I ask this prayer in your son Jesus name.

Write your thoughts:

_____

_____

_____

_____

_____

_____

Affirmation: Today I will think about things that are excellent and worthy of praise.

CHAPTER 23

Chosen

Scripture:

> "But you are a chosen generation, a royal priesthood, a holy
> nation, His own special people, that you may proclaim the
> praises of Him who called you out of darkness into His
> marvelous light;" I Peter 2:9 NKJV

Reflections:

To be chosen is to be among the special, selected people.
We are consistently reminded that we are special people.
We may not fit in. We will likely stand out. We are all different and chosen by God.

My Prayer:

Dear God, thank you for choosing me to complete my
mission in this life. Thank you for reminding me I am not
required to be anyone except me. I ask this prayer in Jesus'
name, amen.

Write your prayer:

_____

_____

_____

_____

_____

_____

Affirmation: I know I am chosen, holy and special.

CHAPTER 24

Wisdom

Scripture:

> "If any of you lacks wisdom, let him ask of God, who gives
> to all liberally and without reproach, and it will be given
> to him." James 1:5

Reflections:

Anything that I do not know, I pray and ask for wisdom. That is wisdom. I don't wonder. I pray and ask God for wisdom.

My Prayer:

Dear God, I am intentionally remembering to pray and ask you rather than wasting my efforts wondering. I know you have all the answers to all my questions. I ask this prayer in Jesus' name, amen.

Write your thoughts:

_____

_____

_____

_____

_____

_____

Affirmation: I will pray and ask God for wisdom.

CHAPTER 25

Do Not Worry

Scripture:

"Don't worry about anything; instead, pray about everything. Tell God what you need and thank him for all he has done. Then you will experience God's peace, which exceeds anything we can understand. His peace will guard your hearts and minds as you live in Christ Jesus."
Philippians 4:6-7 NLT

Reflections:

In my season of worship, I have learned to refrain from worrying about anything. When worrying occurs, it is my cue to pray and worship. When I shift my focus from worry to worship, His peace surrounds me. His peace is my incentive to keep praying and keep worshipping.

My Prayer:

Dear God, I choose to refuse to worry when I should be praying. I choose to tell you what I need and thank you for everything you continue to do for me. Thank you for continuing to give me peace during my storms. I ask this prayer in Jesus' name, amen.

Write your thoughts:

_____

_____

_____

_____

_____

_____

Affirmation: Instead of worrying about anything, I will pray about everything.

CHAPTER 26

Trouble

Scripture:

""I have told you these things, so that in me you may have
peace. In this world you will have trouble. But take heart!
I have overcome the world." John 16:33 NIV

Reflections:

My pastor always says, "Trouble don't last always". He's
right. It's refreshing to know that in God, there's
peace amid trouble. Even when I don't see the way, I do
remember he is the way.

Question:

What's troubling you?

_____

_____

_____

My Prayer:

Dear God,
Thank you for helping me find peace inside my storms. I rest in the fact that you have overcome this world and that you know what troubles me. Thank you for comfort in the midst of it all. I ask this prayer in Jesus' name, amen.

Write your thoughts:

_____

_____

_____

_____

_____

_____

Affirmation: I can find peace even in my troubles.

CHAPTER 27

He Heals

Scripture:

"He heals the brokenhearted and bandages their wounds."
Psalms 147:3 NLT

Reflections:

I find it reassuring to know in my distress and afflictions, God still heals. When I am broken, I have learned God cares about my brokenness. He makes everything right in very wrong space. His assurance gives me hope that everything will work out eventually.

Questions:

Where are you broken? Where do you need healing?

_____

_____

_____

My Prayer:

Dear God,
Thank you for healing my heart and bandaging my wounds so many times. Lord your genuine love for me reminds me to love others as you love me. I ask this prayer in Jesus' name, amen.

Write your thoughts:

_____

_____

_____

_____

_____

_____

Affirmation: Only God can heal my brokenness.

CHAPTER 28

Bless You

Scripture:

"The Lord bless you and keep you; The Lord make His face shine upon you and be gracious to you; The Lord lift up His countenance upon you and give you peace." Numbers 6:24-26 NKJV

Reflections:

First and foremost, I know God wants to bless me. My focus is to stay the course and finish the assignment. I never want to exit a season or situation prior to obtaining what God has blessed me with. He knows my beginning and end. He already knows how he wants to bless me. My challenge is to stay focused on him and how he will bless me in this season.

Question:

How do you want God to bless you?

_____

_____

_____

My Prayer:

Dear God,
I am in awe of how you continue to bless and keep me. I am grateful your face continues to shine on me. Thank you for your grace and peace towards me. I ask this prayer in Jesus' name, amen.

Write your thoughts:

_____

_____

_____

Affirmation: The Lord will Bless and Keep me.

After This:

After 28 days of intentionally reading bible scriptures, prayers, and affirmations, you can continue this spiritual ritual for the rest of your life. Reading scripture daily allows you to become familiar with the promises found in the Word of God. Praying each day allows you to become familiar with talking and listening to God. Affirmations remind you of what you believe about yourself. The purpose of reading this book is to encourage you to spend time daily reading scriptures, praying and reminding yourself of what you can do in this life. How you start will determine how and where you end. I encourage you to continue this spiritual ritual of spending intentional time alone in his presence and watch your progress and maturity propel you into who you are truly meant to become.

CPSIA information can be obtained
at www.ICGtesting.com
Printed in the USA
BVHW041757160223
658686BV00012B/246

9 781662 869914